United States Navy

by Julie Murray

ABDO
U.S. ARMED FORCES
Kids

www.abdopublishing.com

Published by Abdo Kids, a division of ABDO, PO Box 398166, Minneapolis, Minnesota 55439.

Copyright © 2015 by Abdo Consulting Group, Inc. International copyrights reserved in all countries.
No part of this book may be reproduced in any form without written permission from the publisher.

Printed in the United States of America, North Mankato, Minnesota.

052014

092014

Photo Credits: AP Images, Shutterstock, Thinkstock, © Keith McIntyre / Shutterstock.com p.1,
© Official U.S. Navy Imagery / CC-BY-2.0 p. 11, 15, 17, 19

Production Contributors: Teddy Borth, Jennie Forsberg, Grace Hansen

Design Contributors: Candice Keimig, Laura Rask, Dorothy Toth

Library of Congress Control Number: 2013953950

Cataloging-in-Publication Data

Murray, Julie.

 United States Navy / Julie Murray.

   p. cm. -- (U.S. Armed Forces)

ISBN 978-1-62970-097-7 (lib. bdg.)

Includes bibliographical references and index.

1. United States Navy--Juvenile literature.   I. Title.

359.00973--dc23

          2013953950

Table of Contents

United States Navy

The navy is a branch

of the U.S. **Armed Forces**.

The navy protects America from the water. They use ships, planes, and weapons.

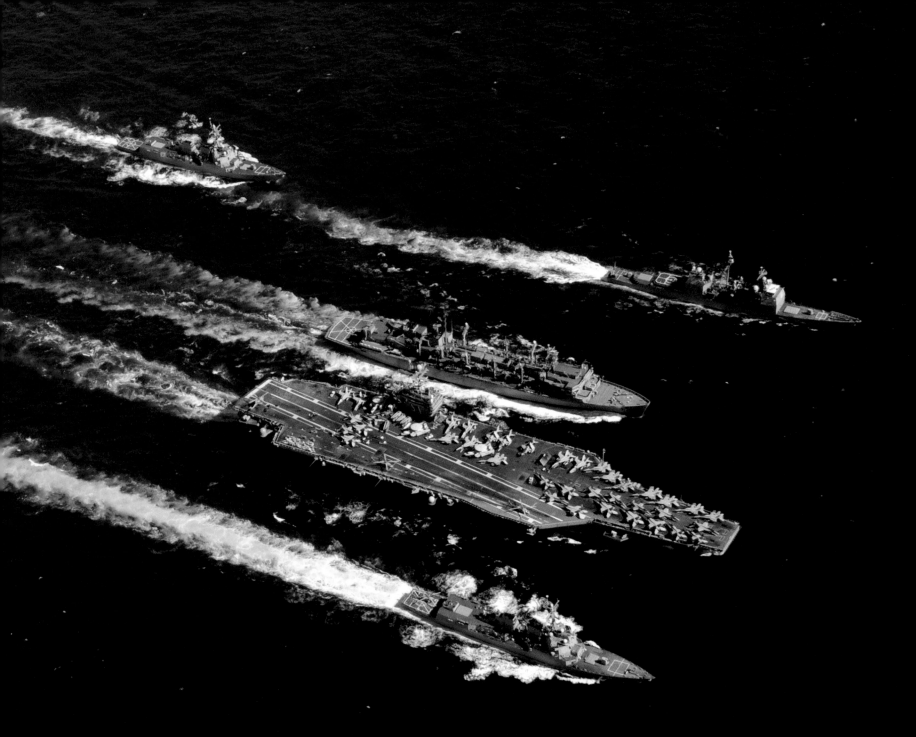

Vehicles

The navy uses many
different ships. Cruisers
are fast **warships**.

9

Destroyers guard the **fleet**. They keep other navy ships safe.

10

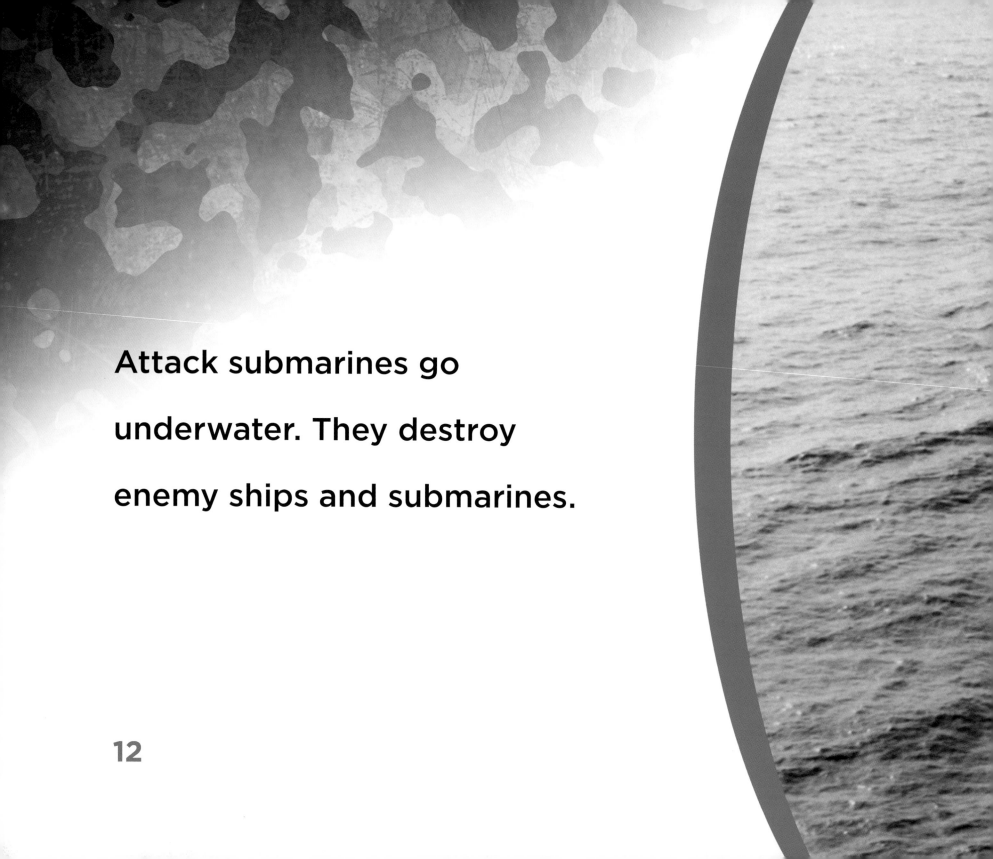

Attack submarines go underwater. They destroy enemy ships and submarines.

13

Aircraft carriers have planes onboard. The planes take off and land on the ship.

Jobs

There are many jobs in the navy. Mechanics fix things.

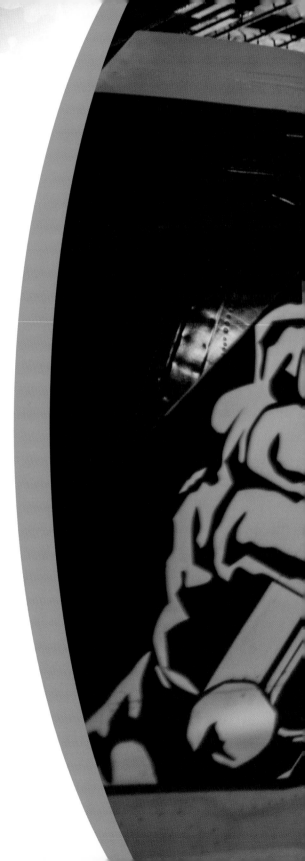

Pilots fly planes. Doctors take care of the sick and injured.

"Non Sibi Sed Patriae"

The navy keeps Americans safe every day!